# BEYOND
## THE BONDS OF
# EDEN

Spiderwize
Remus House
Coltsfoot Drive
Woodston
Peterborough
PE2 9BF

www.spiderwize.com

A CIP catalogue record for this book is available from the British Library.

The views expressed in this work are solely those of the author and do
not necessarily reflect the views of the publisher, and the publisher hereby
disclaims any responsibility for them.

ISBN: 978-1-911596-57-8

# BEYOND
## THE BONDS OF
# EDEN

NIGEL PEARCE

# Contents

# Preface to
# 'Beyond the Bonds of Eden'

Eden was, in Milton's epic poem *Paradise Lost,* a state of bliss, but bliss without that knowledge from the apple on *The Tree of Knowledge* plucked so sensibly by Eve. Humanity must, however, once it has bitten that apple, accept that they must inevitably listen to the raving of Nietzsche's Madman explaining the 'Death of God' as follows:

> *God is dead. God remains dead. And we have killed him. How shall we comfort ourselves, the murderers of all murderers? What was holiest and mightiest of all that the world has yet owned has bled to death under our knives: who will wipe this blood off us? What water is there for us to clean ourselves? What festivals of atonement, what sacred games shall we have to invent? Is not the greatness of this deed too great for us? Must we ourselves not become gods simply to appear worthy of it?*

*Nietzsche, The Gay Science, 1882*

That is the state of absurdity that we must accept if we are to live without illusions. What Jean-Paul Sartre called 'good faith' or authenticity. Not an easy path, but one that any dreamer of beyond the horizon must accept. It is indeed a labour of Sisyphus, but like Albert Camus in *The Myth of*

*Sisyphus* argued, it is the only genuine one. As he argued there is only 'a single serious philosophical problem':

> *The consequences of realization are suicide or recovery.*
>
> *Camus, The Myth of Sisyphus, 1942*

I read Camus and Nietzsche as a young teenager and they affected me profoundly. I then ran away to live in the counter-culture of the early 1970s, broke down and all the other Dantesque madness. However, I have been 'clean' and 'dry' for thirty years and found a salvation in creative writing and academia. I have a BA in Humanities with Creative Writing 2:1, and at present am studying for an MA in English at The Open University. I have mental health issues but live with them, as it were. This collection is looking in retrospect. Who knows what the future brings and we must conclude, argues Camus:

> *The struggle itself [...] is enough to fill a man's heart. One must imagine Sisyphus happy.*
>
> *Camus, The Myth of Sisyphus, 1942*

Nigel Pearce, October 2017

# I am the lost child of Simone de Beauvoir

*I was made for another planet altogether. I mistook the way.*
— *Simone de Beauvoir, The Woman Destroyed, 1969*

An Icarus had flown in those currents that whirl around the disc
of frenzy and Truth,

You were mother half-crazed with that music of Beethoven
which caressed minds,

And where else could that Appassionata Sonata be played but
bliss in our heavens,

A wandering Aphrodite chained to a cruel cross, our love was
crucified and bleeds,

Neither of us was of this world, but we were made of the stuff
dreams are shaped by.


We celebrated our love of poetry and philosophy, you Muse of
past and the present,

My wings had whipped up some tempest as contorted limbs can
towards time terribly,

Until no longer your butterfly heartbeat for me, but drowned in
a sea of golden coins,

An ornate veil hid a petrified perfection, that brute had finally
bought and formed you,

Mind melts and blood runs sour since there is no sacred milk to
nourish nor heroin hit.


I, amphibian without wings, gliding, sliding through endless
pages of waves and books,

Solitary creature shunned by a world, hermit in a watery
wasteland of thesis and writing.

3

# Autumnal

This season of mellow fruitfulness the apples were teeming with termites,

That Tree which held a fruit of temptation called knowledge is now rotten,

An earth where its roots clasp and grasp is frozen like leaden bronze sky.

A howler of hurricanes tossed the loose leaves; laughter was lost so soon,

This woman who kicks her way through the shades of brown and crimson,

Until she flees in a flurry of rustling colour, Eve escapes the Garden gladly.

An Adam lies in depths of a cider vat; he had waved, drunk and drowned,

The leeches replace manacles on his mind and his body is now wormed.

So, in a Universe where time grinds with the motion of mortar and pestle,

The divine is shrunk into tedium of day and the humane was hammered

In a mould which was made of clay cracked and so broken melted away.

## A teenage political prisoner is detained on wards x and y during the 1970s

An older monk on a secure ward also talked of Tim Leary and Che so we colluded,

The nurse without eyes just a film covered one presumed in purveyor of darker art,

A poet wrote in metaphor not grasped by those who had embalmed patients' minds,


Children are born in a bell-jar of discontent but do not worry doctor has the thorium,

But the clientele spat sputum into cardboard spittoons not emptied but flung in rage,

So we were hidden on wards with sycophants, faces like brick and mortar monotone,


A nurse wanted patients to be aborted cherubs of heaven, some were like banshees,

No one commented until the ritual burial of a demon because things are hot in a hell,

Just play bingo pleads Janus the therapist while he winks towards some wincing nurses,


No take over the asylum and make it your campus howls that interned revolutionary,

The patients rise-up like tigers but then the panzer squad prepare a chemical Cosh,

As electro-convulsive therapy was had by all in the aftermath, the wires just buzzed,


Not forgotten were those whose deaths in Stammheim Prison left us with bitter taste,

Bitter is the taste of lemon, lemon is yellow that will colour us if cancer strikes in liver,

But red will be funeral shroud as jaundiced eyes never glazed by cowardice of heart.

# Poem to lost love

*An intellectual is someone whose mind watches itself.*
*I am happy to be both halves, the watcher and the watched.*
*- Albert Camus, Notebooks 1935-1951, 1998*

The worms are in her hair and creep like crazy symmetry of
slurred syllogisms,

Her black and translucent pupils are the corridor back into the
infinity of inferno,

The nymphets were left broken like alabaster dolls sacrificed to
a dumb phallus,

Some gathered their skirts and stole the microdots hidden in
haste but now lost,

Camus stands alone a pillar of stone and utters his words of
wisdom but weeps,

Back in Sputnik I spin trying to keep the letters of R. D. Laing's
*Knots* on a page,

Tumble into a purple zone through a rose garlanded window
etched in her mind,

Put the harpsichord concertos on again please I love them much
Hermes sighs,

The statue of Camus vaporized, Hermes levitated and we went
weaving waves.


I write these words about those days of dreams and wish my
love not died in vain,

We were children of ether who were not of this world,
entombed within its bounds.

# A lightbulb
*(prose-poem)*

He sits in a luxurious sea of crimson cushions observing a solitary lightbulb.

It is suspended, like his mind, by a single cord. This is pulsating slightly, or so it seems; no, it is the bulb flickering. The room, it is like being in a cube of pure

white, is caressed by fingers of light and shadow. The darkness is merging into the dawn which is peeping through green curtains, they are hung on steel wires suspended between two hooks, the Alpha and the Omega. He finds his feet and

glides around the bulb to discover a yellowing square of plastic, here is the switch,

he clicks it off, the bulb is extinguished and so is his mind, it's cast into an ocean of crawling patterns that dissolves into mirrors of soft wax. He locates the switch again, pushes the button on and the knowledge of electricity envelopes his awareness, but the dawn lurks outside, there is the world.

In that place lurk purple serpents with eyes composed of composite deceptions, ice which burns like the Sulphur of hell, flee knowing I am both ice and in this purgatory perhaps

That torn and twisted red heart you see before is not cold or black, it beats too much.

# A portrait of my dead mother

You were confined in this
sorrow,

Standing quietly entrapped by a
drama,

Whose ivy script slowly bound you.
This actress performed before an
audience,

until weeping,

Her tattered mask dissolved
onto
a stage of dust with whispers of infinity.

Our mime was like an ancient memory, a text with
those tears that burnt.

I light a candle,
it flickers in this night of cobweb.

# What a shame

*(In a physical health Medical Centre waiting room)*

Ex-psyche nurse wanders in with an inane grin like he is on gin says, 'what a shame',

You are lucky your enamel is still in place for the Herr Dentist had gouged out mine,

Pull your own daisy but you try that one again and any plastic flower poetry is gone.


Refresh memory on a ward a decade past: 'you will never study philosophy', I have.

Whoops, the phlebotomist says they cannot take that vial of blood you handed her,

You clown minus powder and paint; I am not insane say some in Latin and Sanskrit,


Poor nurse is absent of mind and shame; he is no more than a pain in a patient's brain.

# A poem for William Burroughs

*I saw the best minds of my generation destroyed*
*by madness, starving hysterical naked,*

*dragging themselves through the streets*
*at dawn looking for a fix.*

*- Allen Ginsberg, Howl, 1956*

Staring streets reflect the voids in your eyes which are mirrors
of the squares, they exist without the pricking needle  easing
chaos; you found the  mainline again,

an embrace like an orgasm burning through a vein, Zen with
and without the hassle,

this Light strikes those chemical cells calling calmly to the soul
like the whispered welcome of  nothingness,

The Absurdity is not in these oceans where weeping tranquility
tumbles into dreams

for you were dancing into the masquerades of non-being. High
womb-like peace sleeps, wake, write, weep, fix again.

You survived, died at 83 because being you; you always
'went first'.

# Lines in praise of Sappho

Your heart is aflame like beauty;

With these flowers you garland sacred Helen

Drifting with your bodies and stroking a sultry air of love
flowing between senses, your imaginations of flowers wander
in groves with humming Aphrodite of tears, your voices are
sweet as flutes at dawn the music wrapping your beloved's
body, in her white linen robes of purity and desire, on Lesbos
the Muses sang with joy, to wake a verse of bliss and lyres
do play, but night still wails the song of Rhea. Then Eros had
glanced at them and gasped,

I genuflected dumb before this muse who fragmented.

# Mother, it is not Maxim Gorky

Unlike Gorky the flower of proletarian authorial
voice, this poem will not be like his novel

*Mother,*

It is 4.30 a.m. again; and descent into Hades
has begun because my aged Eurydice is

entrapped,

The Russian dolls within dolls within a mind
must be unscrewed, given a little personal

autonomy,

Orpheus and his *double* Oedipus must descend
and cross the river of the Acheron, a river

of woe,

Gorky saw 1917 blossom so revolutionaries waited
for the wind's howl, the crisis came it was

calm,

Mother is bewildered in Hades proletariat
is dazzled by reflections of

commodities in mirrors,

Not writing *Mother* and no revolution is the
Sisyphean burden for those also expelled from a

heaven.

The ferryman, Charon, undying boatman charges
each of us Orpheus and Oedipus's fee:

it is insanity,

*cont.*

The depths swirl in a twist of whirlpools which
are typhoons of the mind, but he has

navigated across,

Madness possess some incarnations of Orpheus
as children they were hurled out in

blizzards of acid,

Metamorphosis from Orpheus into Oedipus is
ancient like gnawed wormed apple bitten by a

Serpent,

The poet Ovid writes Orpheus abstains from love
of women because things went badly for

him 'no',

The pen is numb and weary of the struggle with
double-demonization of the mind and body,

Reality tears like shoals of piranha fish devour a
pair of lovers, I weep and the sea, the sea

is crimson.

# Two traditional Haiku

# 01

Sun is the fragrance
Of love breathe that sweet scent choke
And live in moonlight.

# 02

Cherry blossom burns
Bright for those it praises weep
We sleep in the frost.

# The day I realized René Descartes was wrong

You were an 'I' who could not pass through the eye of a needle
too wealthy in ideas,

That Doubt of dream games of molten wax, but you were not
an explorer of Psyche,

An ideologue who would never doubt Cogito Ergo Sum along
his preordained Way,

Conjured an Evil Genius to deceive all, the thought of
deception without a hesitation,

Squares become triangles in a Cartesian circle, round and round
you were just dizzy,

Baseline was always going to be Saint Anselm, the proof of
perfection by God alone.


René the rabbits were all in a bag the one you pulled out was
Carroll's White Rabbit,

That day my doubt became an epiphany was when the lie of
Cartesian Doubt died,

An awaking of a lotus flower in the moonlight, rebirth in the
mists of lunacy and love.

# Lines for 'J' (down and out in London)

You, most precious saint of the sacrament from beyond
enlightenment, we had stalked along the pavements of dust that
billowed into our minds,

Core like mine was pure Zen Void tied to the sacred
vein in knots,

A dazed Dionysus with tongue of fire roaring love for our tribe,

Contempt for those swarms of ants that crawl in rhythmic
conformity, Squares within squares, pulsations of
electrical energy

Who preyed on us, prayed for us blind to their encrusted
corruption;

Beloved jive junkie whose crimson sedition is still shouting
from misty eyes,

Down and up in London, still defying that recurring Obelisk of
glinting black stone,

I hope...

## The poet's tasks: a blessing or curse

Still hard at heel, those steel bonds don't bind his mind
like blinkers,

The fire is not to be quenched within his mind and body:
a vocation?

Those flames which lick like lovers probing tongues
cocoon, wrap Him,

But they just burn and erode the being, this is the poet's
grained Fate,

No choice almost like a sort of pre-destination of despair,
myopic  mass.

# Six Haiku

**#1.**

Rust burnt in a mind
It was acid, now teardrops
Explode euphoric.

**#2.**

Corn stood strong golden
Ready for harvest, the rain
You brought left famine.

**#3.**

A heart was made of
Blue glass and beat, but it broke Smashed
like smithereens.

**#4.**

Madness exhales breath
To lift veils, there the sane gasp
For they have no air.

*cont.*

**#5.**

Vampire bat poets

Had sucked your veins, gave them blight

The depths they needed.


**#6.**

Love was spat out like

Spittle, a flute is silent

For it has no reed.

# The Blood-Jet

*Poetry is like the blood-jet, it just keeps on flowing.*
*- Sylvia Plath, Kindness Collected Poems, 1981*

An Apple was offered by that delightful serpent, she snakes into
a syringe as the vein is hit,

Or gushes from the severed artery of a child when hit by
shrapnel, seeps from that cut wrist,

Her brilliance is in the ability to transform any piece of cloth
from pure white to a darkest red,

She flows through every syllable this severed finger slides
across tyranny of the blank page,

She is dripping from the poet's pen in splendid crimson as from
vampire's satiated mouth,

A poet's ink blood is deeper red being contaminated by crazy
cells which is cancer,

He had bitten the Apple offered, gorged upon it but it was not in
the Garden of Eden but Hell,

The Invisible Gardener had forgotten to give him entry to Eden,
the poet fell before the Fall,

Poetry is blood-jet, then anemia leaves these poets prostrate
before the death time wink.

## Two classes, two poetics

A hair and the width of it is all that matters on the scalp because
it is seething like greed,

You need trophies because of all those lost like any myopic
vulture searching for carrion,

That bejeweled pen you posture with runs dry before any ink
oozed to awake blunted nibs.


The nib of the masses is forged with both steel and blood, it has
the sound of thunder clap,

It writes on papyrus, parchment and paper, the internet and is
flexible like a   willow in wind,

We have many pens, you know not all who hold them, some
scribes, sleepers and workers.


One History, two classes, two poetics and a single struggle:
clash of revolution and reaction.

# Poem of a redeemed suicide

An angel had fallen into Grace,

this is the damnation at the antechamber of despair,

Now beyond tepid temptations

he stumbles through the scrub of tangled blind  stares

Of willful unseeing eyes no, blind stares and jealous glares of those who claim to spare,

This baptism is of sand, a font

of dust just like those who are sieves, nothing there but Barbed wire and head holes,

the fruitless bites of those rotten apples make me puke into an abyss which is home

I know it well, here the lotus flower blossoms at 5.00 a.m.

A poet was persecuted by the magicians of modernity the priest purveyors of psychiatry,

His persuasions are portrayed in patterns of ink which we call words not smeared turds.

Their wands are broken on a philosopher's stone which is where the poets learn craft.

# Her book of cold spells

Moonbeams awake again as the White Goddess has crackled into his mind like electricity,

This morning the pen scribbles because a poet's thighs are bound in tight bondage of blue,

A witch had locked the belt some barren desert drifting time ago with her brass prison key,

She peddled tears and fears from a pious silence, her book of charms only cast cold spells,

The bell had rung at birth to exorcize desire from her body that perished in pure purgatory,

Curses were cast in her casket; she gouged out hearts with a lunar crazed cardiac surgery.

To tickle love again would not be my metaphor,

But a rook woman who writes with dark thread.

# The transformation

That saint of sanity is trapped in a glass menagerie of sanctimonious deceit,

Until a flea has penetrated the dome and flies around in search of dog dung,

The master of platitudes swipes the irritant into apparent oblivion with a fist,

A metamorphosis takes place and the black dot mutates into a fluttering bat,

Hideous Beauty is born it crawls leaving a trail of crimson slime on the floor.

Being blessed with a sound mind the saint books a check-up with Doctor Sane,

The shrink with a grin and a wink says you have found your vocation Narcissus,

To be generous I will diagnose you with schizophrenia so you better play a role,

Go and roll into the fetal position because it is medication time says that nurse,

Insanity's martyr lives in an asylum but it is dwarfed by the shrine of Absurdity.

## A latter-day leper

A bug was bagged just for moral sanctimony in a shop of a holy sacred music faith,

It was a case of contagion danger so he is to be pillared as he must be on the fiddle.

No nothing to do with appearance for they know not yes, they do he has the plague.

I have the flu so have this rather large of box of tissues I bought at Boots just now,

We do not want any of that here they say in a jerked horror which is spattered out,

A leper is not in a colony it is clear but is from an asylum, prison or infections unit.

They are so pleased until the parasite speaks and is sprinkling holy water on them,

Exchange complete, money for folk, manna for Mammon, art thou holy hypocrite,

All are children of the bourgeois so germ smiles and says good-bye and they reply.

This poet in amber begins to weep with ink these words for people cut like Knives.

## Another Adonis (upon the suicide of a friend)

Looked in those eyes and saw a galaxy of stars like death's untamable love,

Not beloved Cohen's 'Bird on the Wire' but your words with syllables unstained,

Tigers glancing out of the shadows but always they would purr perfect pulses,

Asymmetry maybe but who wants to be a square, disequilibrium of pure tides,

They would wash us both away into torrents of tremendous terror but tenderly,

Always the day dawned danced its words across our minds, the cloud of light.


A scroll not rolled out for those staid sane pens with their soulless nib scratch,

Our pens etched souls of amber, but words will reverberate like love and loss.

## Haiku

The winter spirit
Smiles, mistletoe whispers but
Always breaks like ice.

## Haiku

This sun shimmered stalks
Of corn pieces wounded flesh
And shed icy blood.

# In the temple of Aphrodite

Shoot

white light in a rush

to entwine in pulsations with the ivy of death,


drown in that heaving tissue

with our shadows of poetic nothingness,
we are cast into hollows


Here banshees

awake us from frozen

dreaminess with their folds of white silk, they sooth our cries


In

temples where those melting molecules
are vibrating, it is here that

we weep with Aphrodite.

## No more will the creatures of Prometheus fail in their tasks

A spark zigzags then you put a hand to cool the heat into this lake and your fingers,

Became frost bitten and they just clawed us cruelly, the reaction we pose does not

Require refrigeration rather a transformation from victims of timidity into blacksmiths

Of molten metal, we fashion steel into objects of collective Nemesis, instruments of Retribution; Once buried and lost until the new vanguard of Spartacus performs acts,


To lance a swollen abscess of pus, it must be drained, the barefoot doctors Inflict

A necessary pain an incision, a wound with History's scalpel, poets don't just wear

The masks of Dantesque masquerade, no; our dreadful dream is a relentless beam.

# The chess board consists of 64 squares, are you one?

The chipped chess pieces, the pawns, chant their abhorrence
at the Smooth and uninterrupted movement of both a Rook
and the Queen, At the fatal power of the King's demise
which terminates their game, He was checkmated because of
impotence and ineptitude, you didn't Avoid being mated: the
Grand Master who is reincarnated as a flea Studies the game,
metamorphosis's himself into sticky brown slime, He then
oozes onto the board, only godless like the inexorable tides,
The tacky mucus seeps its way into the pristine checkered
surface. Did you lead a checkered life or as cramped as the
pawns, chipped and clipped, never raced from A8 to R8, only
P-K4*, an anticipated Opening and so is everything else, just
predictable like the ticking of A chess clock, you 'play by the
rules', 'stay on the board'; secure, its Death-in-life because the
brown snot is caustic, it will erode you until Deranged the only
option is to plead for checkmate, you 64 squares.

# The runaway

Darkness dawned as his swimming sperm and her egg of shell
fertilized in eclipsed dance, this was genesis of the children
who tumble in dust of those goblins glared like death,

They impaled these children upon stakes of plastic prepared us
to become an adornment

Of bourgeois taste that square whitewashed prison-cell
called family,


It begins as they as they hammer those first nails into you the
crucifixion Is by white noise, eyes pierced by glass arrows until
death comes aged six, A body wrapped in a shroud of pins,


The child was resurrected at thirteen; he was beginning to
plough the lime furrow, through fields of lemon, they had
folded into a daze of hazy tangerine.

# Conception in the desert

Jab
a silver
pin into any

Poet and see
sand pours out,

It
flows into
a scratched hourglass

Which
leaks particles through
dream's prism

Into
desert, here
poetry is conceived

With
those relentless sandstorms,
they blind.

# Elegy for Elise Cowen ('beat' poet: 1933-1962)

Your smile is bright with magic, it draws in verse,

To glimpse the 'straights', their vision is blurred,

And gazes inert, that form is carried in a hearse,

But you who danced the naked poetics  preferred


The peace of wombs, the warmth, and
'rush' induced seductress,

Our wastes are frozen with promises, caught and chosen

This moth of candle and flame is burnt and  wingless,

At dawn you're cupped in a wrinkled hand and have written


A dirge of deserts and biting sand which sings into the syringe,
enchantment of the finite 'fix'

Lies with accusations on pages scribed in blotted rings,

This sacred insanity is vibrating your soul, a  matrix


For jewels the wind whispered opiate kiss, its

In here where belief lies on the periphery, the poetry,

Ascends in grace with those from Auschwitz,

You stumble across the graveyards and weep in  symmetry.

## On poets who lose their sanity because of unrequited love

Love

had sweetened tongues

to caress in these dreams of bliss,


Numbed,

this night is enclosed in a cell. The shadows of desired,


Emptiness gaze from the melancholy in her eyes, the poet is cursed by his plague of blindness.

## Winter Haiku

Ice has formed across
A lone pool, words are crying
Beneath its smooth face.

## Haiku written in memory of
## Edie Sedgwick (1943-1971)

Bliss was fixing fire
In shadows, flower of flame You wilted to bloom.

## Haiku on poets

Cut that mind of coils
And it bleeds an ink of joy
That is caught by stars.

## Haiku No. 4

A pillar of stone
Has a cloak of golden It wraps itself in.

## A poet becomes catatonic

A

heart of dust

is fleeing the square of black onto  white?


The

silken veils are drifting into a river of mirrors,

here baptism is transience trapped in a house of tears


With

the Dead, they kiss with burning  words

like bubbling acid which blisters until poetry is left mute.

# A priest realizes God is dead and mourns

A chill
chasm of coldness is beating this heart

Where
once lover's warmth had ridden like dawn,

He
had celebrated
a mass, a libation,

Now
standing stunned in torn vestments

Night
has enfolded
his soul, the sacrificial

Rite
of Winter frost
has frozen his tears into rivers of ice.

## Lines on the loss of love

The poet had gazed into a sky of lime green clouds carved in
crystal, his mind Embraced a sun of white linen, but her Sun
sunk and spiraled before him into a World without those who
love to roam the lunarscape, there poets fix into dream, that
stratosphere is where the fallen angels who touch mind

and body perform their undying ballet of love and lamentation.


The poet's moistened eyes can see only her drama of pain,

he genuflects before her bejeweled chalice,

but its wine has seeped into luminous gutters, here the drunken
poets tumble.

## Metamorphosed

A crown of thorns is encircled by a ring of rose petals,

Its rays are piercing his eyes of confusion, she sits still

And listens to the foaming breath which winds around Her
head like a black serpent, it is contracting, she is suffocating
but pulls at the coils of this twisting snake and begins to heave
and then breathes again, he pulls at the cord and drags it down
around his waist in silence,

He's waiting until the black-backed beetles have scuttled across
their dappled floor, she now begins her chant, a

Dirge to gods of dust and lace good-byes, an exorcism of
Insects, she is metamorphosing and flies out of a window.

## Narcissi and red roses

Gusts of wind are howling around this white cube, our bare
room; I pluck the veils of silver cobwebs from these shrouded,
stinging and bloodshot eyes, a globe of green satin is rolling
around the floor in a mist of purple, at its burning core is a
priestess of Aphrodite, one of those who serve the cult of love
on Lesbos, the isle where Sappho sings her spells.

She begins to celebrate mass, I genuflect before her altar of
withered narcissi, an aroma of sandalwood is weaving like dust
blown across a calm sea, this scent intoxicates our senses, my
supplicant's hands are cupped in the form of a chalice before
her, she is peeling the petals from a red rose, they flutter gently
into a porcelain cup, it shatters into jagged fragments.

## Our Lady of Sorrows in Notting Hill Gate (1973)

That green-scaled goddess of grief how she is wailing from
her brown soil grave, it is here that those recently resurrected
Dead Exchange their laughter without lament, but you, who
are skeletal with yellow skin pulled tight in a smile of delight,
you, a beatified Courtesan who roams these connected and
tuned-in grids, a heart Wrapped in the sackcloth which is worn
by an incipient lover of Chaos, here a frozen embryo begins to
pulsate, it breaths and stings the bitter pulp of that apple bitten
in the Garden of Pleasure, ice folds into our eyes until lost
we're born into this spectrum of zoned silence, I embrace you,
you took the crucifixion from my eyes we weep.

## Oedipus is expelled from Eden

Her tears of crystal are an unbound metaphor dripping from
those silent Pools of his mother's ocean of eyes, Oedipus
glances away, blinded with Pain, picks up a Syringe and finds
his mainline to a tranquility of night. In these depths there is a
shadow dance of desire and Oedipus is tied to the mast for this
voyage into a zero, Sirens, lovers, mothers and the Madonna
are the poetry,

Their nectar is sweet to taste, his tongue touches moist Petals
and caresses with the relish of finite  whispering.


But the Inquisitor gazes down spewing us from an Eden, we
were beatified with a band of light around our heads, but a bond
of thorns is formed which pierces both mother and son, so now
roam an interminable lunar  wasteland.

# Hymn to the mortality of the Nazarene

The Void beckons like graves welcome the dead, she weaves
barbed Threads of wire, dark mystery, to coronate the poet who
paces forward to glance into an infinity of broken glass, her
eyes of smiles

in circles of black staring from a bed of rippling folds, here she
washes the blood from sheets, these stains are bled in a cycle
of betrayal and love, sunset and Sunrise, he wipes the tears of
mortality from his eyes and steps to look beyond the edge, a
taunting precipice. He howls 'Father, Abba, why did you leave
my corpse to Hang among unclean men and these anemic
women? Mother, why wasn't it your blood which mingled with
the blood flowing from my wounds in hands, feet and side? You
blessed the wisdom of fools, that myopia of deserts'.

This infant, the Lamb, is a man tuned into those pulsations
Of Alpha,

he leaps into the Void to dance with the damned.

## Psalm to the poetry of joy

The moon rises like mist distilled from a burnt river to whirl
with her humming until the bonds unravel, now she is caressing
her smile into radiant morning, her dust is lingering it sprinkles
onto dormant souls of night awaking our song of love to a
golden dawn, the poet's pen is dipping into this chalice of
nectar, we wander across pages with infinity and innocence a
dance with the light and shadows of sacred ritual, Psalm of joy
to a pristine

      moon and the drowsy  sun.

## She is the bridge across the river of Death

A vulture sweeps on hidden currents seeking carrion. We
cuddled death and squeezed it out of a rock; the vibes began
gliding around a hill of lush green grass overshadowed by

A Gold Phallus.

The phallus ejaculated the words of the dull with a force that
shot them high into the

sky where glazed eyes are blind, drilled them into the side of
the head where dilated

pupils are gobbling madness into their depths and then a pink
fish gulped their dirge.

Flying beyond the cruel clasp of fire and reaching the icy shady
spheres where there

was a river of sparkling glass which was fluid and flowed fast,
a woman clothed with black robes approached, her face was
deathly pale and her eyes dark and sad, she said: 'take my
hand', we floated on and skimmed across the surface of the
river that sparks,

her whisper is melody: 'this is your end, dissolve atom by atom
in my tunnel of night'.

# The broken mirror
*(a journey into the subconscious of the poet)*

Those eyes of a mistress at dawn cloaked in silence, staring into
the hollow vision of his sight like night, the poet, ancient like
crazed Oedipus cast in marble, burn with those licking flames
melting these colours,


Sucked into this still lake of mirrors, wind blows the butterflies
in this star gazed flight, now we are  ebbing


into tactile darkness soothed by dusty lunar wandering.


This mirror is shattered by the incessant beating with hail, Frost
clad poetry swallows glass, we're stumbling  Adams.

## Dreaming of the Muse

On Poetry
sweetest tears are wept,
Caressing the shadows of silence this
Muse is ancient as Electra;

She whispers breath onto a tissue
psyche,
which vibrates like a web of
gossamer:

Dream with shifting sands like a
vortex of voids.

Doves with broken wings who fly
from a cage,
scribe those poems of night which ache
with love's sorrow.

# Prometheus lives just outside of Babylon

echo

baby

groover

Babylon

dreamer,

drowsy

demon

fixing

with

Prometheus

bound

in her

silken

lemon

robe.

# The writing of verse with night

The poet of night's desert begins to scribe

like waves into an ocean whose mist is without dawn,

Drifting across these fields with wonder, like the touch into
swaying seas of corn and sun, sigh with the lovers


Like oceans, their caress is dripping like wax and breath onto
paper flowers, swirling into an endless spiral of clouds.


Moonshine weeps into this ocean of nothingness, the dust is
like a masquerade which is dissolving into white and zero,


Their masks melt, softening into visions like the oblivion with
eyes shining, shadows like insomnia with dreaming.


Spring's dancers wander across the virgin page with its sighing,
this is a word beginning to form into a wave, a whisper of sand,


The cloaked pen weaves into this morning shimmer of cobwebs
in which the Muse hangs suspended like eternity caught in ivy.

## Poem without a title

No existence

without language no journeys

without those words to

Prepare self for

this trip in

imagination

A

voyage deep below dive into

the Abyss that underworld

it is here that we write with our  demons.

## The Steppenwolf

A wolf wanders the Steppes in a dance of solitude,

The deserts of snow stretch interminably, glistening

Expanses without a horizon, his eyes are burnt by rays

Of sun which burrow into a heart woven of silk, freedom is the price Paid for his emancipation, this Escape into a wasteland is Anonymous, tracks left soon melt for he leaves no mark, the only mark is the one that cuts his heart and from which there can be

      no escape.

## Two poets contemplate Salvador Dali:
### *The Persistence of Memory*

Her mind is opening like a
lotus flower stung

By a spear of steel,
her breath drifts in lemon

Globules, pupils are fixed on the
door which is woven

From willow branches, he opens an
aperture to discover

A zone which interacts
with her black eyes, leaden

By the mist of lunar storms, they
embrace, bodies are like

Cotton pages blown across a sea covered in silver
scales, until wrapped

In a ball of silk, they exhale rhythmically
with the pulse of the Earth, the clock faces have melted.

## To oblivion

That mistress with melancholia is sitting like a
consumed Buddha

        in my prison cell,


Holy tears are wept dry here descending into a fathomless

              verse,

           Feel the breath


but never the caress of her soul,

     Intimate with the finite of vacuums whispered like night.


The Inquisitor pierces this haven

        with voids melting our eyes


of glass which are pristine with weeping, footprints in
the sand are

     swept away in waves of oblivion like spirals of hollow.

## To Art

The Void, its cloud has rain, a spring to quench our
sight, to damn and pierce the pain,

But art is fire in flight.

# Lines written in melancholy

Sweetest death

you are the goddess of summer  nectar,

The honey for the poet to drown in unconsciousness, verse is prostrated before you, both in mind and body: Holy One,

Holy Oblivion, Holy

Death.


We, the children of the soul's catacombs scribe our ink onto virgin paper,

The white page glances shyly, trembles a little, anticipating the

pen,

A nib begins to weave tapestries of willow meaning,

these are cloaked in the shrouds of images floating
along a stream,


       we are wandering through this labyrinth of  poetry.

## Dylan and Caitlin Thomas drink themselves into oblivion

Let us dance with our dream of death,

Grasp tightly together, tumble in tunnels,

Chanting to nil, to cloaked zero, to chaos,

Until freed from this frenzy of whirling fire

We're stroked into sleep, a slumber of solitude.

# Introduction to Experimental Poems No 1-6

*Poetry, 'stream of consciousness' writing*
*and 'Beat' culture spontaneity*

This introduction examines the historical and theoretical context in which Experimental Poems: No 1-6 were written.

A method of writing which was developed with Freud's theory of the unconscious became known as 'stream of consciousness.' It was an attempt to penetrate the great subterranean ocean of the unconscious. This writing was characterized by an inner monologue which was:

> *The direct introduction into the interior life of the character*
> *- Édouard Dujardin, Les Lauriers sont Coupés, 1887*

Hence the reader would, by a free flow of language, gain access to the unconscious world. James Joyce and Virginia Woolf are examples of 20th century writers who combined 'stream of consciousness' techniques with realism. They wove complex patterns of language which were inspired, to a considerable extent, by Freud's discoveries regarding the nature of the psyche. The relationship between ego and id was of interest to those who would explore the mind for the raw material of literature.

Like all 'stream of consciousness' writing, these poems are an attempt to 'tune in' to twilight areas of awareness which are inaccessible through conventional forms and, therefore, to illuminate the id, the unconscious.

In an essay written by Allen Ginsberg, a 'Beat' poet entitled: 'Abstraction in Poetry' he suggests that the poet:

> *Reduces the artistic medium to its essential properties*
> *- Allen Ginsberg, Abstraction in Poetry, 1959*

This could, he argued, be the poetry of 'pure sound' (Ginsberg, 1959) like some of the Dadaist poets. However, for Ginsberg, writers such as William S. Burroughs created an abstraction not merely of 'pure sound' but, also, with the energy of an 'altered state of awareness', the vibrant condition of 'pure mind' (Ginsberg, 1959). Their work exhibited the negation of a consciousness which is enslaved to the perceptions of the ego:

*The sensation of self-elimination of all being into the*
*unconscious is the experience of pure poetry*
*- Allen Ginsberg, Abstraction in Poetry, 1959*

In his 1959 essay, mentioned above, Ginsberg describes William Burroughs' writing as:

*A noncommittal transcript into words of a succession of*
*visual images passing in front of his mental eye*
*- Allen Ginsberg, Abstraction in Poetry, 1959*

However, the most significant aspect of writing, for the 'Beat' authors, was not their opiate induced dreaming, but the technique of spontaneous expression which was inspired by listening to improvised jazz:

*To sketch the flow that already exists intact in the mind*
*- Jack Kerouac from Allen Ginsberg,*
*Abstraction in Poetry, 1959*

So, in conclusion, these poems are an attempt to transcend ego awareness and swim in a sea of unconsciousness by employing the techniques of experimental poetry to open the doors of perception.

# Experimental poem: number 1

Caressed
the echo of a void
embraces reverberation,

Ache
descends in a river breaking
the clasp of mind.

We are engulfed in this swimming of the id
being tuned for a birthing of primal mother, She
wept with the stroking of acid droplets those
have been caught in a leaking chalice.

These eyes are dissolved with a flickering of
colours that is a still pool in the twilight.

# Experimental poem: number 2

Poetry
lives in a crystal
teardrop,

It
is here that worms
burrow

Spewing
like the earth retching
lava,

Clasped
by the mind manacles
slicing

the body into daylight and the darkness,
night is whispering with her misty breath.

# Experimental poem: number 3

Sand just

flows

through a honeycomb mind,


Ideas

are blown

across an iridescent wasteland


dissolving into an ocean of beats,

we throb, a pulse with this blood


wept

in eyes

cried for wandering poetry,


Descend int

swarms

of crawling echoes


like the dissonant rhythm of chaos.

# Experimental poem: number 4

Tied
to a stake,
this ravishing of fire

Caresses
the free thought
of the shrouded solitary mind,

Heretics
burn in their emancipation, the
purity of our conflagration

Caresses
the cruel laughter
of a celebrant who is mocking

us, we sing in the finitude of our damnation,
visionaries, we are incarcerated in the flames.

## Experimental poem: number 5

White light
licks into an abyss
with the touch of totality,

the
tongue draws a kiss
murmuring with redolence,

this is eternity with whispered dew,
begin our sobbing like a dried lake, the
butterfly is caught in morning flight

wrapped in a veil, his temple of mediocrity, she
is beginning to scribe oceans of lemon, here
night and its burning tears are coaxed

into humming, the drowsiness is like twilight.

# Experimental poem: number 6

The lunar chasm
of verse
free with association,

ivy acid
dissolving the page into
running plagues of

caged rats,
wire trap-door is opening
onto the desert

as masks are cast in rivers of clay,
the smile of a bemused mystic at night,
she is writing with those caustic tears of fire

to be entranced in the cloudy liquid of dreams, spike is
eased into the mainline as infinity beckons.

## She said: 'love is not enough'

Stole
a ticket
to her theatre

Danced with this
ballerina of hurricanes.

Dropped words into
her bronze head

That
sparked, enflamed and
revolutionized

Her
nails dug into taut skin

Leaving rivulets of
tingling red liquid

Which flowed into
my bamboo pen.

I
wrote lines
of love welcoming

Her
lunar landscape,
Here we wandered

With
Molotov cocktails
primed and ready

For
encounters with fascists
or renegades.

But she became a reactionary, interrogating consciousness,
examining my arms like a drug-squad officer.

She said: 'You've got a needle-mark...a needle-mark from
last night.'

I replied: 'That was the only opportunity to visit my friends, the
only chance to get away from your tight tangle. Yes, there is a
needle-mark, we shoot bliss it's called white light white heat.'

*cont.*

So, lost in
wastelands of ice.

Here
is where
poets and artists

Freeze
their colours into
brittle webs

Of
nerves and
then sever them.

The
tragedy
is acted out

we are tossed away on howls of orange wind into a welcome
green trance.

## 'Mainlining' whilst meditating on a crucifix

Solitary

the moon is weeping crystal,

Welcoming

grey clouds which are a caress

For her eyes

glazed like glass spheres,

The dialogue is with silk veils

like the nothingness which beckons death

into twilight, we are tossed into whirls of dust.

He rolls up a shirtsleeve

the needle marks are like stigmata,

Brown and purple bruises that glare

as shadows weep across the terrain of whispers.

Glancing heavenwards

our light is dancing into the voids of night,

Silhouettes are roaming around this room, the Word

is suspended on a cross of wood, emaciated bodies are
sacrificed to this fire which is never to be quenched by the dew?

## Lines on William Burroughs' concept of 'death-in-life'

Square
hearts had
stopped, they were

Just
rusty bilge
pumps, someone turned

The switch
off,
what a turn-on

Never
dug that
scene with America

And
atom bombs,
chant with those

Of
us who
have a different

                    sound

                              and

                                        song

to the hooded-snake death dirge, breathe an autumn

                                        wind

                              of

                    pure

                              purgation,

          howl

                    cathartic

          baby     burnout

          buzz     madness.


          He had placed
          enigma in caps.

                              opened that cap, cooked it,

                              fixed it, again, again, hazy.

DECONDITIONED HIMSELF FROM
STATE SUBLIMNIAL MIND MANIPULATION,
He had the sweet-death golden flight of Icarus, also the endless
labour of Sisyphus.


                    Illusion, allusion and delusion.


Crimson crystals are burning

                                        *cont.*

pulsating

embers

gobbling

Inferno,

is this a solitary illusion like blood?

stained

sacred

Sacrament

or an academic allusion to a sanitized

Dante,

mistaken

because

Although this may not scold your flesh

forget us

Damned

At your peril purgatory will not cleanse

you, Hell

is where

we weep wild like galloping horses, just snorting this chaos, the

delusion is that heaven existed, no haven or home for us.

# Speaking of viral poetry...

*Language is a virus from outer space...The author is simply a
node on a network, through which ideas pass.*
*- William Burroughs, The Ticket that Exploded, 1962*

That fatigue can no longer frighten us like the ice sheets in the
mind, it is beyond any vestige or manifestation of fear as glaring
of sun drills eyes.


The black petals begin to fold inwards

when a gaze is or isn't fixed, tangles of twisted thorns of a tight
thistle bush are forests of emptiness, viral poetry is written and
formed into lakes of ice, from ice is refined the pure crystals
that are polished into those old cold stars,

they had imploded long ago creating the gulping black holes,
babies' mouths who drink from a black nipple which oozes dark
milk, it's ancient not nectar, it is the ingestion of the 'Other', us
as dark subject, objectification is unmade.


Promenaded people you wake up and don't think black holes
are empty, scabby fingers are grasping the bourgeois hand and
it shivers with revulsion, grey suited exorcists wail 'demon get
out', but we existed for eons before Eden or logos; our word
is an infectious virus. For you are totally helpless, we have
convinced your best philosophers since Epicurus and inspired
the poet Sappho, then lit the fuse around October 1917. We
are the Virus made word, made material in your universe, we
are cellular.

## Some variations on a theme of unrequited love inspired by reading William Carlos Williams

a).

In autumn

wind blew golden leaves like her sorrow.


b).

Have drowned

in her lunar silhouette

to wander in our shadow.

# Lines on Brigitte M
*(a leading member of the Socialist Patients' Collective)*

A chill and steel grimace glares and stares
from the tarnished goblet from which she

                                        didn't drink.

Substitutions are easy in class struggle,
she didn't substitute emotions with zeros

                                        never drunk,

Replace the proletariat with a vanguard?
but never replace authenticity with shit

                                        of oppression.

Kill a revolutionist with a gun or tablets
but they will rise like your fear of death.

                                        Many drunk

From this cup with Brigitte M, not china
tea-services of the oppressor; she smiled

                                        then gulped

That red wine of love, it intoxicated her
with a fantastic desire to destroy Daddy in
all his manifestations.


She was an incarnation, a realization and
beatification of insurrection, her gun fired

            lemon butterflies

                    of

love.

# Summer of love
*(a villanelle)*

Time melts; we thawed a frosty reality to dissolve ice with
our love, Our eyes whose dilated pupils could swallow any
hardened gaze, (You fell across this hallucinogenic Cosmos,
these stars tumble).

We crucified the betrayal of damned love and stared to humble
That dark spark, we conceived this just like evaporating into
haze, Time melts; we thawed a frosty reality to dissolve ice
with our love,

I touched with delicate fingers the clasp on your eyes to
unbuckle A stream, the purple fragrance of humming, a goddess
was ablaze, (You fell across this hallucinogenicCosmos, these
stars tumble).

You crumpled into a sphere of sighs encircled by white light,
a dove whose wings were caressed as we dived into the sun in
a daze, Time melts; we thawed a frosty reality to dissolve ice
with our love.

Our song was vibrating into weeping trees, nectar dripping,
suckle Each other's ancient milk which is a sacred libation with
soft praise, (You fell across this hallucinogenic Cosmos, these
stars tumble).

Tangerine gasp intertwines in a frenzy of breath, it falls from
above, Then we lie exhausted in a grave, our bodies consumed,
but raised. Time melts; we thawed a frosty reality to dissolve
ice with our love, (You fell across this hallucinogenic Cosmos,
these stars tumble).

# The creation myth of Purusha in the *Shatapatha Brahmana* (c.800BC)

Our minds may try and cancel, attempt to blank, this switch
was flicked 800 B.C., he had over 1,000 eyes and heads,
Purusha was total visual, complete sight, absolute cognition:
dived into night without oblivion.


But a core of zero he only became a number through
introspection, digging that nothingness until he floats Around
a crown of Lotus flowers, here he discovered the warmth and
softness which is Yoni, he luxuriated

'I am.'

But like poets at dawn without a pen and paper he had only
desire, he tore himself with pure golden energy to Create
'Other', lover, she became a daughter, they were black and
white flaming water and running fire: joined.


This act created you and you and me, so says this myth.
Ashamed she ran like a gazelle fleeing a lion, he would Become
a gazelle, again and again he deceived her until they had
produced each and every animal on this Earth.

## Psalm to the poetry of joy

The moon rises like mist distilled from a burnt river To
whirl with her humming until the bonds unravel, Now she is
caressing her smile into radiant morning, Her dust is lingering it
sprinkles onto dormant souls Of night awaking our song of love
to a golden dawn, The poet's pen is dipping into this chalice of
nectar, We wander across pages with infinity and innocence A
dance with the light and shadows of sacred ritual, Psalm of joy
to a pristine moon and the drowsy sun.

# Your eyes are shining
*(a prose-poem)*

Those eyes shine with emerald green in our trip again, it has
the certainty with which a frost in winter will freeze a blade of
grass and is sure as a decaying autumn leaf of gold is trampled
under the boots of eternity. But, my goddess of the lunar
wailing, your perfume intoxicates the psyche of this poet as
he is falling into a labyrinth of dreams. Here shadows are like
obscured glass splinters which pierce the mind, we are cast
into a fallibility of chained genes, they hang like globules of
honey draped on a derelict hive. It is here we return step by
step, through the honeycombs, past the corpses of dead worker
bees to the queen who nestles her sterile eggs and beyond to the
primordial swamp, there our stunted fingers clutch each other in
a grasp of love. Your eyes are still as we come down again, so
softly into our folds of tissue.

# A meditation on Andy Warhol's Factory

Many had entered this company of the joyful and mad because
they wrote and did speed enticed they were sucked into a dark-
room, dragged in but

Spewed out when in pain; some fixed and wrote, others painted
after a hit, There were those who wailed their ink or paint onto
paper like orgasms of A moon's second rising: some were
green-eyed with their claws extended

Scratching each other in the desert and simultaneously drunk
from an oasis.

Their profane families of distrust were crucified and sacrificed,
coffined permitting poets to descend from their cross without
that burnt stigmata.


Some wandered and wised their way out, went to labyrinths of
communes as hashish somnambulists, but alert they kept a pen
and paper within reach.


The barbiturate bard taught to fumble, stumble and mumble
proclaims:

'I can recall and write about the verse they wrote in his
Methedrine Ark'.

## An incarnation of Sappho and her friend accidentally OD

Some spit with spite and call it love, but not us, Not in a temple
of Aphrodite, here Sappho tends A flame which brushes her
lips, they are burning And red…now purple as the heroin
hits hard like A hammer thumping its heat up the arm into
that Galaxy of welcoming brain cells, the hypodermic Hangs
limp from her arm, I gently draw the spike Out of the bruised
vein, her arm flops diagonally Across an orange cotton shirt,
I clean the syringe By rhythmically flushing water in and out
and Finally squirt the crimson juice into blue china Bowl; next
prepare my hit, we uncurl in a temple Of Aphrodite which is
where lovers can purr softly,

the floor opens like a gaping mouth and swallows.

# A man became an egg
*(surrealist poem)*

There was a spectral man who hid in a physical frame,

he roamed like a grounded vulture across anonymous plains of
concrete, there is no harvest of golden corn or pleasant deer to
inspire the poet here, only the arched

acridness of the hard, the junkies huddled in alleyways wailing
with junk sickness: once a thin and translucent

membrane formed herself around the man and he just touched it
tingling rebirth, she shyly encrusted herself

but

     egg

        shells

            are

               thin,

                  egg

                    boxes

never are quite right like papier-mâché disintegrating

in the rain, the shell shattered and she madly distorted herself
and became his yoke: both essence and burden.


An artist with eyes like black oceans painted the egg in
beautiful gold, blue and bright crimson: he ate the egg, yoke
flowed out dark as bitter blood into the pen of the poet who
writes as a serpent who has just been uncoiled.

# The ice-box

This is a box within a box, a world within a world, a house which is typical of many found within suburbia. It is brown bricked, anonymous and almost transmits hymns of praise to some tarnished copper god of mediocrity. In the kitchen of this house stands a fridge, it looks white and prosaic.

Open the fridge door and at the top on the right is a sky-blue ice-box, it has three white stars to confirm the adequacy of its freezing capacity. Inside the ice-box is a rectangular tray which is divided into squares, each can be filled with water and then frozen to produce the perfect ice-cube. This can then be dropped into a frosted pink glass which wraps around it, add fruit juice and there is the perfect chilled drink.

A son frequently opens the fridge door and pulls down the sky-blue ice-box flap and peeps inside. He examines the frosted walls which, paradoxically, burn his fingers; they are almost burnt with the coldness. It is in this world of ice-cubes that he discovers another dimension which exists separately from, but is intrinsically attached to, the ebb and flow of everyday life. The son's mother had died some years ago and he had been left the house, he did not sell it because there wasn't anywhere else to go. The son had an unusual relationship with the ice-cubes in the fridge finding great comfort in popping two out from the tray and holding them in his hands until they were numb and the ice-cubes dissolved into water.

The living-room of this box within a box was bare, no carpet, no furnishings or pictures. However, glaring at him was a gas fire. It had short brown steel legs with one at each end to support it. A copper pipe stuck up through the floor boards and was connected to the fire. The fire itself was coloured in two tones of brown, light brown at the bottom and around the sides of the gas jets and above was dark brown. The shelf which was on top of the whole apparatus and rested against the wall had white plastic knobs at each end, one is to turn on and ignite the gas and the other is to control the flow of gas to regulate the temperature. This fire concerned the son greatly, it almost dominated him. He didn't like the hissing of the gas or the flickering flames and the brief smell of gas at ignition caused him much anxiety. He felt little or no choice but to constantly check and check again that the gas was burning correctly and there was no leak. With the certainty of the tides his life became enslaved to this gas fire. The only respite was allowing the ice-cubes to melt in his hands.

Just as the season's motion is inevitable the gas fire developed a leak. Fortunately, the son was elsewhere when the explosion tore through the house destroying it and its anonymity. It no longer looked like all the other houses in the cul-de-sac. The fridge was badly damaged and thought to no longer fulfil any useful task; it was taken to the local tip. The ice-cubes turned into water, but a more profound metamorphosis took place: a voice said:

'My son, there is no longer any need to worry.'


The water had leaked from the ice-box and out of the fridge into the rubbish of the tip in which it germinated a seed planted at the beginning of Time. The shoot will push its way up through the waste and bloom next spring, a snow-drop.

## Psychiatric nurse, try reading some Dostoevsky

The psychiatric nurse wears a smile of roses, But when he opens his mouth only the thorns Show, they rip into us as mercury is rising up the Thermometer, but we are like mercury, we are The messengers of words, of communication Between mortality and the void, our emotional

Temperature is wrong, our perceptions are askew, So chant the nurses as they prostrate themselves Before an idol 'THE SELF' in its glory and feel one

Of the few, a mental health professional, we break the Shackles on the nurses' ego and drag them from their Shallows of grey bourgeois murk, then of course they React and start behaving like enflamed flamingos, with Moments of insight here, incisive understanding there, and then in wonder a diagnosis: nurse read Dostoevsky And step into the weird world of us underground people.

# On Anne Sexton and her fellow confessional poets.
*(a Shakespearian sonnet)*

Her hands began to write a page with dew,
Those hearts had shed the haunts and bonds of light,
She turned and smiled to cast a spell, this guru
So tense until her pen began to write
A verse of storms, angels of night that share
Her seas of lavender wept waves of wonder,
The sun had raised so red to kiss her hair,
She sat quite still and breathed like Buddha
Her wine could sweeten bitter potions
But doctors, priests of modernity,
Were glaring flames, her poems were emotions
They tossed to Hell with shocks of electricity,
This burnt into these hearts of love, the mind
Was numbed by barbiturate and lay blind.

# Dreaming of Morpheus and William Burroughs
*(a Petrarchan sonnet)*

We groove along furrows to cut the wet pavement,
This street reflects an inner web, this glassy maze,
The path to oblivion, it melts like an echo of praise,
The temple begins to sing with awaking ferment, The
dream-powder, its magic is like night's scent,

A garden of delight where sight and tears are glazed,
You spike the mainline again; this is not so crazed,
The cobweb is caught like a dream's finite content.

But Morpheus is a cruel god, in darkness confess
His bonds, we know his mellow, like a nocturne We
were naked, our mind's flow to be dissolved, A cloud
whose rain which beats us nails, Venus

Always burns away my colours in eyes not taciturn,
What remains, the riddles of thought, never told?

## A poet is sedated in a mental ward whilst contemplating death

Embrace lunar death

of the most Holy beatitude,

You're swirling

with particles of dust


in winds,

Darkness has sung

without light again like pacing seasons,

This lamb

is sacrificed on an alter


draped with staring eyes,

A chant of hollowness rises

from the pulsating mass of communicants,

Their empty eye sockets

where love has been condemned


By supplication,

they genuflect and weep with tears of ice

as the poet is prostrated and given an injection of
chlorpromazine.

# A psychiatric nurse gets writer's block

The nurse tightens as his bow bends back to
shoot arrows of poetry into folds of sky,

That vampire is sucking inspiration from us
patients, he falsely claims the tradition

Of Dionysus as he roams the ward, a giant glaring
into our dormitory, we have hidden

Our words and pens in the secret place, here

We also store stocks of medication, kept just

In case of emergency, the tablet is stealthily licked
under the tongue, retrieved and then

Hidden in a crack behind my bed, the nurse's bow
has snapped and his arrows fall upon us.

# H

H is for Hell,

H is for Heroin, H is for Heaven, H is for Helpless,

H is for Hopeless, H is for Homeless,

Should have been aborted and lived in the safety of a bell jar.

S is for Schizophrenia, S is for Solitude, S is for Suicide.

Fled fragrant suffocation in Eden for the bitter taste of
brown sugar.

# On glimpsing Gudrun Brangwen in 2009

An Aphrodite whose skin was smooth as alabaster hums along
the pavement, daring V-back dress, she is hoping to meet
her Dionysus who is embarked on the same sacred mission
acted out each generation, tonight is Saturday night just like
the last one.

> school is like mind freeze pressure
> from examinations pressure from
> the curriculum pressure from
> ambitious parents.

Those minds are like tender plants, they need earth to grow but
they are treated with pesticides, they are being maimed. It was
the parents who were expelled from Eden and not the children,
yet the children must roam a bone scattered desert.

Aphrodite and Dionysus drop a few pills, gulp down some
booze and dance their ballet of the senses...they hope she
'Comes on' next month. I caught a glimpse of Gudrun today her
eyes were fire yet ice and kissed the sun with full delight.

# A priest realizes God is dead and mourns

A chill

chasm of coldness is
beating this heart

Where
once lover's warmth
had ridden like dawn,

He
had celebrated
a mass, a libation,
Now
standing stunned
in torn vestments

Night
has enfolded
his soul, the sacrificial
Rite
of Winter frost

has frozen his tears into rivers of rivers.

# Laboratory Experiment No 2

Red tentacles are gripping the wasted wail of a seething brain
which writhes in delirium with $C_{10}H_{15}N$ rush, white light;

eyes hang loose attached only by yellow threads to grey
sockets, they melted a millisecond ago and now are
dripping, dropping

by diamond drop into a culture dish, the doctor makes a smear,
places the slide beneath the lens of a microscope and peers
in, a child yells into her eyes, she jumps back too late as the
laboratory rotates into concentric circles, it has become a
phantasmagoria

$C_{10}H_{15}N$ is the formula for methamphetamine (Methedrine).

## For poets who lose their sanity because of unrequited love

Love

had sweetened tongues

to caress in these dreams of bliss


Numbed, this night is

enclosed in a cell, the shadows of desired


Emptiness

gaze from the melancholy in her eyes,

the poet is cursed by his plague of blindness.

## An itinerant poet and a lover celebrate Mass

A shimmering of shadows is pulsating from his
crown of lemon light, this has encircled with
rays the waves

Of matted hair, slowly this exorcism of disbelief
begins, he is stroking the gold bond of slavery
from her finger, a breeze is caressing the sands
from a forlorn temple into the red tints of
mortality, an electric shock shoots through their
grid, he bows before her mass of black forest,
genuflects like Adam before Eve's temptation,
they dissolve into ascensions of dazzled love,
she is smiling and elevates the Host before him,
they feast.

# Abel gets paranoid?
*(a psychological study of Cain and Abel.)*

Abel is trying to run but clinging dreams
enfold His mind, then caught without motion
and maimed

By silver darts of fatigue, he sinks and
screams out: 'No stop please': tumbling like
a dice down a lime Mountain he has lost
those bleating sheep, dazzled by eyes of
glowing ruby which spit like drops of a


Bloody reverie, tears cling to his fingers like
Swords Of Yahweh, whimpers: 'Cain?', who
replies 'cool man,

It's alright now I've killed Dad; we are free as the birds'.

# Blood and Water: the most ancient sacraments

In oceans the waves can look choppy and boats seem tossed like flotsam, but dive deep down into the depths of these seas and there lurks a rushing current which can suck a person into a zero, drive you into insanity like a mob devours its victim who like themselves is a wept victim, vicissitudes cruel as the sea, so here in these black blind bloody depths are flows that can only be revealed by the poet; but psychiatrists claim a similar trade.

Oedipus had loved his mother, this is the way of oceans, but when she was like a branch and snapped like her sea son, then damnation roared. Oedipus was never freed, love cannot ice, and the sea chains are ancient like tears and fears: tranquility was new, not deeply grooved and a pyre was fanned like the prayers of St. John of the Cross, fire howled by wind

It burnt Oedipus, so he returned to the familiar sea of zero where he lives as a shy amphibian, there is no blood of Clytemnestra and Electra in this water.

## Song to the oppressed: 'never trust men in suits'

A howl encrusted with sores and dressed in the persuasive
vestments of An abomination slips from those contracting grins,
that is the priest enrobed

In the cloak of an abortionist greets the pleated wail of another
cocktail party, Another nightmare, so let them cruise in their
seas of dollars and moral excrement, Beware you anachronisms
because the lava of the oppressed is beginning to bubble, We
say: 'No shit you pigs, we're going to sweep away the dust
from your theatre', You entombed bourgeois whose ballet
of cardboard replicas is step, step, stepping To the toiling
of a Death Bell, it is beginning to ring in their ears and they
wince with

Fear, our hammer, the mallet of History is striking their skulls
only to reveal a vacuum, Never trust that pinstriped suit smile;
it's obscured with clouds and in terminal decay.

# The cobra and the poet

The
cobra didn't
wear a uniform,

It
slowly lifted
a swollen neck
which
was ripened
with venom, yellow

Eyes darted and
smiting tongue flickered,
Jaundiced
fangs impregnated
a trembling troubadour


With the poison of conformity, the poet felt nausea then stung
revulsion: He roams across urban Steppes and lives with
wolves to howl their words.

## A child recollects his mother's self-harm and then writes a poem

The poetry of bonds had tightened around his throat, Those muscles which muzzle a heart were learnt in Blizzards of sharpened scalpels, her piercing ice, a child Had crawled into a ball so tight to forget the cut, it oozed Blood and burnt still warm into his head; her ruptured Drama would never cauterize, instead it pulsed with the Deism of a marauding herd of ghostly horses galloping Into a mire of black syrup, this had stuck and dripped in Globules from his crown of fake thorns which he threw Into the cauldron to brew with her tainted breath, they Inhale this scent until the pen writes in strokes of blood.

# Hippie woman in a North London squat, 1973

A chick
is sitting in silence
within the broken shell of

An egg,
her radiance ripples
around the room sinking into

Beds
Of rose petals, now
her gaze begins to penetrate the wall, white light is
flickering
out of his hollow sockets of nil,

His
murmurings are staring,
but she moulds that lava surge

Into a
river and is deflecting
energy into a collapsing circle, wrapping her breath in lace.

## Caliban is reincarnated as a snake.

A cobra lay dazed and coiled, with glassy fangs he injected
waves of electrification into molten blobs of wax, this serpent
was sliding in a fog of disinfectant around suburbia with
hooded amber eyes, they glow, He hangs without the chains
of slavery which burden that place, is poisoned by toxicity of
blown innocence.


We left the funeral in boxes,

could only free ourselves from the cemetery of echo by escape


to LSD psychosis

to amphetamine dependency to heroin addiction

to organize the proletariat

to advocate the armed struggle

to celebrate the sacraments of schizophrenia.


Poets wonder at love that blows like ribbons into infinity, but
write in cauldrons where the pure of Hades are  floating.

# Let us dissolve demons with poetry
*(lines for poets trapped in a ferment of the Inferno)*

They pierced us with an ice thorn and claimed it was their crown of thorns, No love, then write about it,

Blisters of fatigue burn minds and bodies with their claws of phosphorus, No love, then fright about it,

Comrades have been driven like cattle stumbling into the bloody abattoir, No love, then fight about it,

Counter-culture dreams drifted into that deep and dark well of Narcissus, No love, then cry about it,

Cannot adore because serpentine cobra had spat into sad eyes and blinded, No love, then die about it.

Let us dissolve the mocking

demons WITH OUR

POETRY

NOW.

## The spirit of Ulrike Meinhof addresses
## the bourgeoisie in 2009
*Ulrike Meinhof 1934-1976*

Our waves will wash away the
    sand into a sea, Bourgeois
    fuckers your system
    is screwed
        Ripped off the poor and the tenants,

A hot and dry summer will scorch with fire and now burn
baby burn.

    Think you are stable...no just sinking into
    an ocean of Narcissism which is not pretty,
    never learn bourgeois, Now your houses are
    being repossessed and the mind Twangs:
    those robbed of their dreams awake you
    shake in your shoes as the ghettos buzz,
    start to tremble...you have failed and now
    the revolutionary Nemesis waits.

The Angry Brigade is aware and alert and the Red Army
Faction has not forgotten, Socialist Patients' Collective flexes
their minds and their trigger-fingers;

Do not think the Red Brigades are all banged-up inside.

    Our waves will wash away the sand
    into a sea, Bourgeois fucker
    your system is screwed
        Ripped off the poor and the tenants,

A hot and dry summer will scorch with fire and now
burn baby burn

## Storm and Desert

The fiery worms which burrowed into my mind,

Are like the maggots which are eating the soul,

Now they have died, drowned in a dark ocean,

Which raged until evaporated by the biting sun?

That tempest has lulled and my thirst has abated.

## MIND CLOCK

Integrating like the hands of a clock,
Pointing to the misty time of no hours,
Which passes its breath in the silence?
Slowly returning to the house of a self,
Here are shifting sands, a wilderness,
And the clock has melted with a heat,
Forget to tock in time with their Rhyme.

## Morphine Love

A morphine angel stroked my mind,
As a mother rocks her child to sleep,
And a lover touched the soft breast,
Like dew on the grass in mornings,
No chaos, just the gentlest whisper,
Love between sheets of dark death.

## Heroin

I shot a dream up my aching arms,

In a haze of mind just lost in a skull,

Calling names from my quivering lips,

Pastel shades soothed weeping eyes,

Heaven strolls like floating lilac lilies,

In that caressed pool of emptiness,

Forgetting the anguish of our hunger,

Go those thunderclaps in our minds,

We were at peace a dewy humming.

## It is alright babe

The needle pieces that loving vein,
Like Love smoothing a lover's hair,
The white-heat rushes up our arm,
Into welcoming minds like sunrise.
Cruising with sleep forgotten eyes,
I watched 'the Man' as he grinned,
He had shaken-up into the kitchen,
Nobody else has clocked his move,
I just rise and stumble gaining focus,
Walk with amphetamine confidence,
A crookery-high piled shooting room,
Gently approach and smiling, saying,
'It's alright babe, give me that knife,
I have Valium in my pocket so relax,
Swallow four of them with water, relax.'

I groove back into the music room,
He finds my lost vein and another hit,
Tears have burnt farrows into my face,
It was alright babe, because of Valium.

## Gather the Fragments

Like a brown and ruddy crinkled autumn leaf Blown,

Swept by gales, tempests and storms,

While others gushed like the chilliest hurricane,

Demand you will experience equally the puss Perpetually

Like considering a mirror

This will crack with the intensity of stares.


Who will gather those fragments?

# Breakdown: seeing beyond

Seeing beyond the tokens of things,

To just penetrate the masks of men,

And to lift the veils of women reveal,

Looking beyond a child's tears, sobs,

To see a screaming devouring mouth,

It could rip a communicant from wine,

Hurling them all into a Dantesque fire,

Of forgotten selves and dream ghosts,

Who roam the ploughed, frosty fields?

There she glistens in that lunar-sea,

Will she melt in the winter sunshine?

# SHE

Woman is the manna on the breeze,

Woman is the wind that plays chimes,

The hands that play and stroke a harp,

They welcome like warmth, shy, sharp,

Respond with moonbeams on the lips,

The memories conjoined never separate,

She is the stream entering green oceans.

## She mutilates the temple of her body

My body has become a twisted shrine,

Is a tube of paste that is oozing slime?

It must be cut to allow the pus to flow,

The knife straight blade purges wrath,

This is incense to be inhaled by them,

Intoxicate them like a cyanide pellet,

She, the ultimate soliloquist departs.

## A warm woman and a cold girl

Grooving along a cold pavement,

Taking poems to a warm woman,

Cold girl just leers across a street,

With her harsh stems of corn hair,

Her eyes are dead, she is an advert,

Those ruby lips, mouth something,

A shallowness of mass magazines,

Not like a flowing river-fire woman,

Who reads and writes lunar poetry.

# Today

The poets languish in the mental hospitals,
The criminals are running the government,
The poor live in concrete boxes or streets,
Mind-control priests celebrating the Mass,
We weep from bruised, blackened red eyes.

## Before the incense was lit

Before they lit their choking Incense,

He was

Dammed before the beginning of Time,
Fated to shed tears like autumn leaves,
Cursed to be blown by the hurricane,
Doomed to be drenched in raged rain,
Blighted at birth to be a series of selves.

A temple has been desecrated by fools,
Even before incense was burning scent,
At the Farewell, let there be no lamentation.

# Hermaphrodite kiss

He had wept as the nappy-pin jabbed him,
He had hidden behind sofas feared at six,
He found shelter in a syringe and bottle, 12.

The Minotaur had roared without any control,
Careered through the labyrinth stabbing horn,

Like a twinkling moth he Immolated on flames,
Adoring the collapse of his veins and stigmata,
Choreology in the darkest oceans of the moon.

We mutants offer a hermaphrodite midnight kiss.

## Sleeplessness

Walking through these cold nights of bitter sleeplessness,
My being slid down the dust pipe, a Way of Nothingness,
Images become distorted in a mirror of caustic Absurdity,
These are both within and without no escape they shout.

Will any kind of peace, wipe my clay body, feverish brow?
Will the whisky-bottle or the syringe be a cloth of comfort,
Just to hush, hush this chaos that burns like hell in mind,
And dissolve the soul to stop the cancer eating my body.

This barrenness of spirit with the potency of emotions,
They cut like a missed arrow of love pierces the heart,
Lead to a desired death or a wilted bed of rose petals.

## No walls, no floor

There were no walls of haven in a family,
And certainly, there was no heaven ceiling,
No solid earth floor to stand upon or walk,
It was sub-terrain world of misty shadow,
It would with certainty of sunset explode,
A fiendish and hellish land of like Inferno,
Where all were tormented by their demons,
A family where no family ever could coexist,
I was born no self, a Tabula rasa smashed.

# On the scene

Look whose back on the Scene man,

Lay some dope on him, be cool man,

A little acid tunes him to the frequency,

Give some speed to wake-up a brain,

Do-him-up with smack to get a habit,

Look whose back on the Scene man,

O.D. Off the scene is blue he is dead.

## One

That slimy silence is just deafening, The Void,
Pregnant with a meaning, We, I, and all the
People in my head, are mirrors of all potential
Pathways, through chaos and the atoms of self,
A social consciousness is just isolation,
Strangled by the honeysuckle of lover's
Woven nets, a betrayal of the revolution.

## Two

A baby is weeping in a storm cloud, A
prisoner on the rack is screaming, The
parents rock to a belted climax, Another
baby born into The Inferno, And the parents
beat their breasts.

## Three

A tempest crested wave crashed on his shore,

Like the rhythms of the sea eroding a coastline,
Suddenly his body is flung up into a blazing sky, Soaring
with swallows on the wind's wild current, Aware of the
finite with the sea and its roof of sky, Only to embrace
the hummed Mass in his cranium, Police came and
smashed, crashed down a door, He, a swaying cornfield
routed the thought-police, To recruit them to the
revolutionary proletariat aim,

A sea is bashing his mind until free he flies away.

# Five

I, like a chick who is emerging from an egg, wanting not
to be born, it has been ordained, In this farmyard with
that choking dust blown, He, she, they are all pecking
around for corn, Just to survive to exist in this yard that is
hard, The farmer does not feed us chicks properly.

Farmers will not let these to live as they wish,
For this is the generation of the battery-hens.

## Seven

Still yet a living frame without a soul, A fire
ignited by the Earth's pulsations,
Lost youth travelled in a zigzag tonight, Still
trapped in a maze yelling for help, A man is
caught in the breeze, no farm, Only the Owner
within ploughs his field.

## Eleven

The memories return in the asylum with breakdown trough, as

when a woman lies with her newborn, no father to be seen,

I wander through fields of gold swaying corn and think
of snow, But

Mozart stepped across the terrain of the self and the universe.

## Inside my skull

Within the cave of one mind,
The skull of Dante's disciple,
Roam two evil men, who shout,
They both accuse me of devilry,
One contorted group therapist,
One a policeman with a baton,
They are stones within a soul,
They are beyond an exorcism.

## Angie Baby

She has worn a blue wool dress besmirched with coffee stains. Buttressed against the cold and the World with jumpers and a belief in witchcraft. She hummed with delight and rose-coloured blushes when her breasts were caressed with holy lips of a prophet. Her heaven roamed across her flesh as his tongue darted and teeth nipped. Only to drown in a sea of esoteric sighs. I loved her with my soul, relished her body if not the mind, I had lost mine. We twinkled across the fields in the moonlight. Until consumed we lay and slept in reveries. The police found a poet in a graveyard one frosty night, he was insane and awaiting a Resurrection of the Dead.

# For Sylvia Plath

I am resting in your grave of nettles,
Your purple soul weaves its entrance,
Like an enchanted violin it is played,
By the nectar breath of your mouth.

My living willow is in a sullen tomb,
It is alight with colour and matter,
It is animated by wandering sighs,
Flowing in a purple force, my blood.
So, you stroke like a lover, my pen,
I write on pages midsummer frost.

www.ingramcontent.com/pod-product-compliance
Lightning Source LLC
LaVergne TN
LVHW091305080426
835510LV00007B/382